Zodiac Signs

SAGITTARIUS

by Elizabeth Andrews

WELCOME TO DiscoverRoo!

This book is filled with videos, puzzles, games, and more! Scan the QR codes* while you read, or visit the website below to make this book pop.

popbooksonline.com/sag

abdobooks.com

Published by Pop!, a division of ABDO, PO Box 398166, Minneapolis, Minnesota 55439. Copyright © 2026 by Abdo Consulting Group, Inc. International copyrights reserved in all countries. No part of this book may be reproduced in any form without written permission from the publisher. DiscoverRoo™ is a trademark and logo of Pop!.

Printed in the United States of America, North Mankato, Minnesota.
042025
082025

THIS BOOK CONTAINS RECYCLED MATERIALS

Cover Photo: Splendoura Prints; Shutterstock Images
Interior Photos: Getty Images; Shutterstock Images; Wikimedia Commons
Editor: Tyler Gieseke
Series Designer: Laura Graphenteen

Library of Congress Control Number: 2024948382

Publisher's Cataloging-in-Publication Data
Names: Andrews, Elizabeth, author.
Title: Sagittarius / by Elizabeth Andrews
Description: Minneapolis, Minnesota : Pop!, 2026 | Series: Zodiac signs | Includes online resources and index
Identifiers: ISBN 9781098247942 (lib. bdg.) | ISBN 9781098248482 (ebook)
Subjects: LCSH: Sagittarius (Astrology)--Juvenile literature. | Archer (Astrology)--Juvenile literature. | Zodiac--Juvenile literature. | Astrology--Juvenile literature. | Astrology--Charts, diagrams, etc.--Juvenile literature.
Classification: DDC 133.52--dc23

*Scanning QR codes requires a web-enabled smart device with a QR code reader app and a camera.

TABLE OF CONTENTS

CHAPTER 1
Meet the Sagittarius! 4

CHAPTER 2
History of Astrology 12

CHAPTER 3
The Traveler 18

CHAPTER 4
Charming and Honest 24

Making Connections 30
Glossary 31
Index 32
Online Resources 32

CHAPTER 1

MEET THE SAGITTARIUS!

Sagittarius is the ninth zodiac sign. People born between November 22 and December 21 are Sagittarians. When people ask for your "star sign," they are likely asking for your sun sign. This is the zodiac sign the sun appeared in at your birth.

Holly

WATCH A VIDEO HERE!

ZODIAC CALENDAR

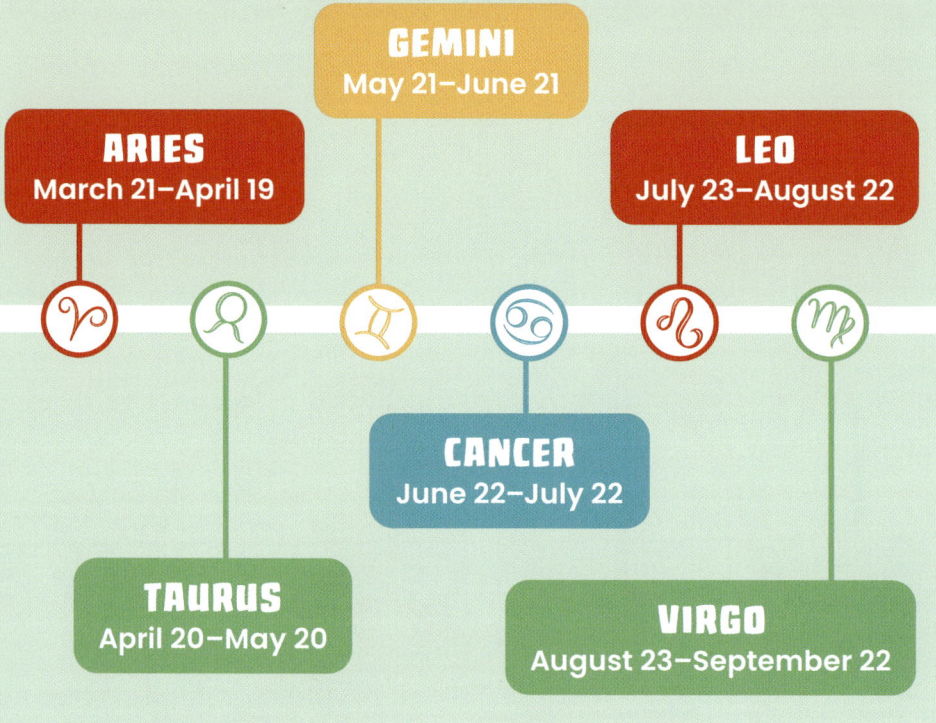

Three features help describe zodiac signs. Signs can be masculine or feminine. Each zodiac sign is given a mode. The three modes are cardinal, fixed, and mutable. Each zodiac is also

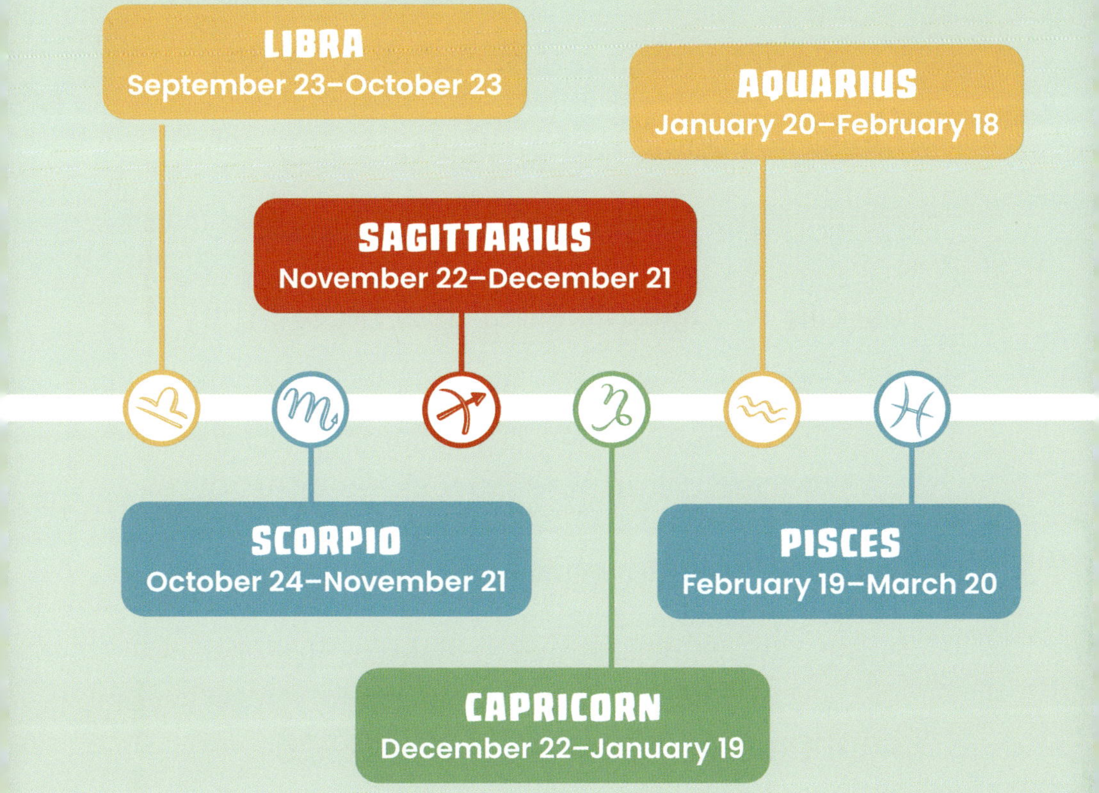

LIBRA
September 23–October 23

AQUARIUS
January 20–February 18

SAGITTARIUS
November 22–December 21

SCORPIO
October 24–November 21

PISCES
February 19–March 20

CAPRICORN
December 22–January 19

a fire, air, earth, or water sign. No zodiac signs share the same three features.

DID YOU KNOW? Mutable signs mark the end of seasons. Sagittarians in the Northern Hemisphere are born at the end of fall.

Sagittarius is a masculine, mutable, fire sign. People with masculine signs are reasonable and action focused. They usually say exactly what they mean. They are outgoing and strong.

Modes determine how signs interact with the outside world. Mutable signs are open-minded and comfortable with change. They are usually easygoing. Sagittarians are active and exciting. They are often bold and dramatic.

Turquoise has been used in jewelry for thousands of years.

Being a masculine sign does not mean Sagittarius is a boyish sign. It is just a way to describe how Sagittarians act.

Chiron helped many great Greek heroes on their journeys.

Sagittarians are **represented** by an **archer**. The archer is a centaur, or a half-human, half-horse creature. Some ancient Greeks believed the archer was Crotus, the son of the god Pan. Other ancient people thought the archer was Chiron, a very helpful centaur.

The Sagittarius constellation is also called Centaurus.

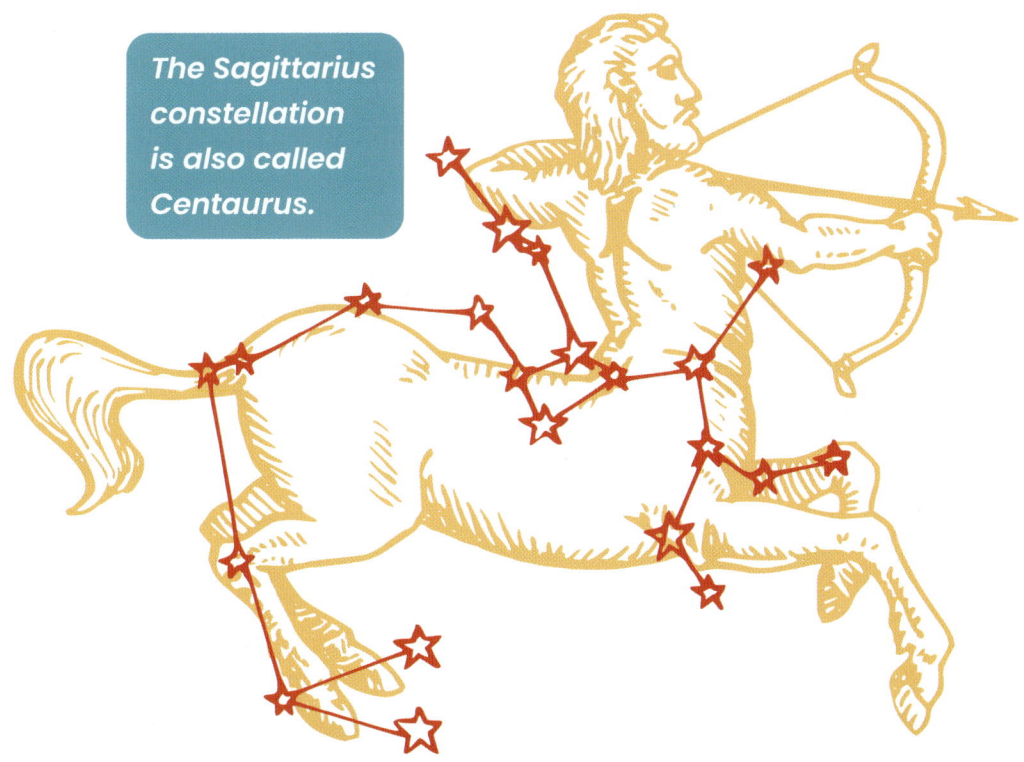

CHAPTER 2
HISTORY OF ASTROLOGY

Humans have searched for life's **spiritual** meaning since the beginning of time. They often looked to the stars for this. Astrology is the practice of reading the movements of planets and other **celestial** bodies and connecting them to life on Earth.

LEARN MORE HERE!

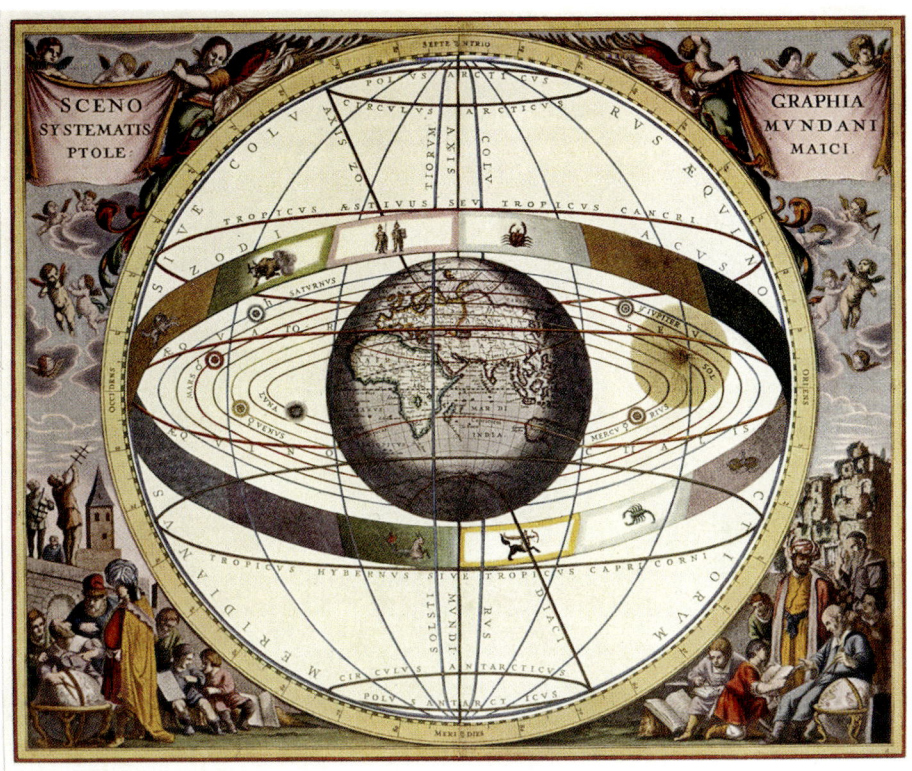

Some ancient people used the zodiac signs to predict future events.

Babylonians invented the zodiac in Mesopotamia over 5,000 years ago. Mesopotamia was the first known civilization. Babylon was one of the region's largest cities.

Ptolemy was an Egyptian man who studied the stars.

Earth and our solar system are in the Milky Way galaxy.

The zodiac is a belt of space around Earth that has 12 well-known **constellations**. Ancient people noticed that the sun seemed to move in front of these constellations throughout a year. The sun spends about a month in each constellation.

The constellations in the zodiac belt are Aries, Taurus, Gemini, Cancer, Leo, Virgo, Libra, Scorpius, Sagittarius, Capricornus, Aquarius, and Pisces. Together they make up the 12 zodiac signs. They are all **represented** by different **symbols**.

Islamic astrologers created new ways to map and measure stars.

THE ZODIAC WHEEL

DID YOU KNOW? Most zodiac symbols are animals. The ancient Greeks called the belt of space *zodiakos kyklos,* or "circle of animals."

CHAPTER 3

THE TRAVELER

Sagittarius is ruled by the planet Jupiter. This is the planet of good fortune, **optimism**, growth, and plenty. Jupiter is the king of the Roman gods. The centaur is connected to Sagittarians because of their wild nature and love of thinking.

EXPLORE LINKS HERE!

> Sagittarians have a love of traveling and exploring new places.

The brave Sagittarian will likely try exciting activities on their adventures.

Sagittarians are curious. They are constantly searching for wisdom and challenges. Sagittarians like to discover new things and places. Most Sagittarians are independent. This drives their adventurous spirit. Sagittarians look at life as what it can be instead of what it is.

Sagittarians trust their own luck. When going to new places and trying new things, they believe that something wonderful can happen. Sagittarians are often in the right place at the right time. They seem to flow easily through life no matter where they end up.

GREAT OUTDOORS

People born in Sagittarius have a love of the outdoors. It connects to their love of adventure and independence. When they are out in nature, they feel free from real-world stresses. Sagittarians also love a physical challenge or activity. It makes them feel like they are living life to the fullest! Sagittarians are most at ease when they know their next adventure is around the corner.

Sagittarians get some of their luck from their ruling planet, Jupiter.

The most important thing to a Sagittarius is freedom. To avoid feeling tied down, Sagittarians will choose hard paths, jobs with less money, or even towns where they don't know anyone. They often make big life decisions quickly, without thinking things all the way through.

Sagittarians can be hard to count on because of their continuous movement and new ideas. They also get into bad

DID YOU KNOW? Sagittarius is the sign of philosophy and higher thinking. Sagittarians enjoy exploring new ideas and subjects.

Philosophers study big questions such as, "What is the meaning of life?"

moods when they feel stuck. But these moods pass quickly thanks to their belief that good things are ahead.

CHAPTER 4
CHARMING AND HONEST

Sagittarius is considered the most likable zodiac sign. Sagittarians are often high spirited. They are funny. They are kind and open-hearted friends who trust easily. Sagittarians are willing to help their friends without expecting anything in return.

COMPLETE AN ACTIVITY HERE!

Taylor Swift is a Sagittarius. She was born December 13.

Sagittarians are great at encouraging their friends to try new things.

Sagittarians can have trouble sharing their feelings with new friends. They worry it will lead to attachments to people or places. If that happened, Sagittarians would lose the freedom they value most. They wouldn't be able to chase adventures whenever they wanted.

People born in the Sagittarius sign are honest. They are direct and always share what they think. Sometimes their statements are hurtful. However, Sagittarians don't mean to cause harm. They are just being truthful. On the other hand, Sagittarians get their feelings hurt easily.

Sagittarians are good storytellers. They often have a collection of tales from all their adventures.

DID YOU KNOW? Sagittarians get along best with the independent and adventurous Aquarius.

The Sagittarian way of communicating makes them very **charming**. They would do well in jobs such as writing, publishing, or acting. However, Sagittarians can also be hard to trust in workplaces. They may struggle following through on projects. But they have grand ideas and want to make the world a better place.

Publishers put out books, magazines, and other written projects.

Today, astrology can answer questions about an individual. People use astrology to understand who they are and why they might do what they do. It can also help people understand others in their life. A zodiac sign can point out personal skills, possibilities, and **internal motivations**.

WHAT IS A BIRTH CHART?

Each person's birth chart contains all the planets in our solar system, the moon, and the sun. The location of where each **celestial** body was based on the exact time and location of a person's birth can be marked on a birth chart. A birth chart can explain even more about a person than what only a sun sign can. The placement of each planet affects the drive of a person. This reveals personal motivations. Astrology experts can read birth charts.

MAKING CONNECTIONS

TEXT-TO-SELF

Are you a Sagittarius? If so, do you think the sign matches your personality? If not, what do you have in common with Sagittarians?

TEXT-TO-TEXT

Have you read any books about the other zodiac signs? How were those signs similar to and different from Sagittarians?

TEXT-TO-WORLD

With the help of an adult, look up famous Sagittarians. Pick one person and write a few sentences about ways that person shows Sagittarian qualities.

archer — a person who uses a bow and arrow.

celestial — having to do with the sky or outer space.

charming — very pleasing and delightful.

constellation — a group of stars that forms a pattern.

internal — of, relating to, or being on the inside.

motivation — something that makes one want to do something.

optimism — the belief that there is always hope for something good to happen.

represent — to stand for or be a sign of.

spiritual — having to do with people's beliefs in things such as the soul, nature, and what happens after death.

symbol — an object or picture that represents something else.

INDEX

archer, 11
astrology, 12, 29

birth, 4
birth chart, 29

career, 22, 28
centaur, 11, 18
constellations, 15–16

dates, 4

element, 7

fire sign, 7–8

Greeks, 11

Jupiter, 18

masculine sign, 6, 8
Mesopotamia, 13
mode, 6, 8

nature, 21

relationships, 24, 26

traits, 8, 18, 20–24, 26–28

zodiac belt, 15–16

DiscoverRoo! ONLINE RESOURCES

This book is filled with videos, puzzles, games, and more! Scan the QR codes* while you read, or visit the website below to make this book pop.

popbooksonline.com/sag

*Scanning QR codes requires a web-enabled smart device with a QR code reader app and a camera.